**MSCHOLASTIC**

D1549583

# writing guides

## With interactive resources on CD-ROM

# Poetry

WITHDRAWN

### for ages
# 5-7

Jean Evans
and
Francesca Kay

# Credits

**Authors**
Jean Evans and
Francesca Kay

**Development Editor**
Marion Archer

**Editor**
Sarah Sodhi

**Assistant Editor**
Tracy Kewley

**Series Designer**
Anna Oliwa

**Designers**
Paul Stockmans and
Liz Gilbert

**Cover Illustration**
Mark Oliver

**Illustrations**
Mary Hall and
Mike Phillips

**CD-ROM Development**
CD-ROM developed in
association with Infuze Ltd

**Mixed Sources**
Product group from well-managed
forests and other controlled sources
www.fsc.org  Cert no. TT-COC-002769
© 1996 Forest Stewardship Council
FSC

Text © 2010, Jean Evans
Text © 2003, 2010 Francesca Kay
© 2010 Scholastic Ltd

Designed using Adobe InDesign

Published by Scholastic Ltd,
Book End
Range Road
Witney
Oxfordshire
OX29 0YD
www.scholastic.co.uk

Printed by Bell & Bain

1 2 3 4 5 6 7 8 9    0 1 2 3 4 5 6 7 8 9

**British Library Cataloguing-in-Publication Data**
A catalogue record for this book is available from the British Library.

ISBN 978-1407-11260-2

**Acknowledgments**
The publishers gratefully acknowledge permission to reproduce the following copyright material: **Marian Reiner** for the use of the poem 'Catch a Little Rhyme' by Eve Merriam © 1966, Eve Merriam. Copyright renewed and reserved; **Nick Toczek** for the use of the poem 'Ten Green Dragons' by Nick Toczek from *Dragon's Everywhere* by Nick Toczek © 1997 Nick Toczek (1997, Macmillian Children's Books).
Every effort has been made to trace copyright holders for the works reproduced in this book, and the publishers apologise for any inadvertent omissions.

**CD-ROM Minimum specifications:**

| | | |
|---|---|---|
| Windows 2000/XP/Vista | Mac OSX 10.4 | |
| Processor: 1 GHz | RAM: 512 MB | Graphics card: 32bit |
| Audio card: Yes | CD-ROM drive speed: 8x | Hard disk space: 200MB |
| Screen resolution: 800x600 | | RM CC3 |

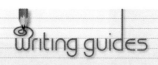

# Contents

# Introduction: Poetry

The *Writing Guides* series aims to inspire and motivate children as writers by using creative approaches. Each *Writing Guide* contains activities and photocopiable resources designed to develop children's understanding of a particular genre (for example, fairy stories). The activities are in line with the requirements of the National Curriculum and the recommendations in the *Primary Framework for Literacy*. The teacher resource books are accompanied by a CD-ROM containing a range of interactive activities and resources.

## What's in the book?

The *Writing Guides* series provides a structured approach to developing children's writing. Each book is divided into four sections.

**Section 1:** **Using good examples**
Three text extracts are provided to explore the typical features of the genre.

**Section 2:** **Developing writing**
There are ten short, focussed writing tasks in this section. These are designed to develop children's ability to use the key features of the genre in their own writing. The teachers' notes explain the objective of each activity and provide guidance on delivery, including how to use the photocopiable pages and the materials on the CD-ROM.

**Section 3:** **Writing**
The three writing projects in this section require the children to produce an extended piece of writing using the key features of the genre.

**Section 4:** **Review**
This section consists of a 'Self review', 'Peer review' and 'Teacher review'. These can be used to evaluate how effectively the children have met the writing criteria for the genre.

## What's on the CD-ROM?

The accompanying CD-ROM contains a range of motivating activities and resources. The activities can be used for independent work or can be used on an interactive whiteboard to enhance group teaching.
Each CD-ROM contains:
- three text extracts that illustrate the typical features of the genre
- interactive versions of selected photocopiable pages
- four photographs and an audio file to create imaginative contexts for writing
- a selection of writing templates and images which can be used to produce extended pieces of writing.

The interactive activities on the CD-ROM promote active learning and support a range of teaching approaches and learning styles. For example, drag and drop and sequencing activities will support kinaesthetic learners.

## Talk for writing

Each *Writing Guide* uses the principles of 'Talk for writing' to support children's writing development by providing opportunities for them to rehearse ideas orally in preparation for writing. 'Talk for writing' is promoted using a variety of teaching strategies including discussions, questioning and drama activities (such as, developing imaginative dialogue – see *Fantasy Stories for Ages 9–11*).

# How to use the CD-ROM

Start screen: click on the 'Start' button to go to the main menu.

This section contains brief instructions on how to use the CD-ROM. For more detailed guidance, go to 'How to use the CD-ROM' on the start screen or click on the 'Help' button located in the top right-hand corner of the screen.

## Installing the CD-ROM

Follow the instructions on the disk to install the CD-ROM onto your computer. Once the CD-ROM is installed, navigate to the program location and double click on the program icon to open it.

Main menu screen

## Main menu

The main menu provides links to all of the writing activities and resources on the CD-ROM. Clicking on a button from the main menu will take you to a sub-menu that lists all of the activities and resources in that section. From here you have the option to 'Launch' the interactive activities, which may contain more than one screen, or print out the activities for pupils to complete by hand.

If you wish to return to a previous menu, click the 'Menu' button in the top right-hand corner of the screen; this acts as a 'back' button.

## Screen tools

A range of simple writing tools that can be used in all of the writing activities are contained in the toolbar at the bottom of the screen.

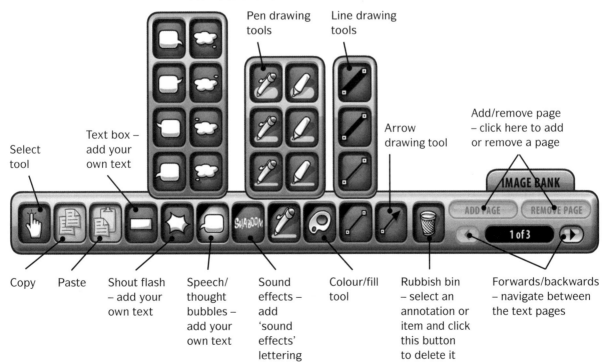

Pen drawing tools

Line drawing tools

Add/remove page – click here to add or remove a page

Arrow drawing tool

Text box – add your own text

Select tool

Copy   Paste   Shout flash – add your own text   Speech/ thought bubbles – add your own text   Sound effects – add 'sound effects' lettering   Colour/fill tool   Rubbish bin – select an annotation or item and click this button to delete it   Forwards/backwards – navigate between the text pages

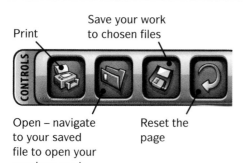

Print

Save your work to chosen files

Open – navigate to your saved file to open your previous work

Reset the page

## Printing and saving work

All of the resources on the CD-ROM are printable. You can also save and retrieve any annotations made on the writing activities. Click on the 'Controls' tab on the right-hand side of the screen to access the 'Print', 'Open', 'Save' and 'Reset screen' buttons.

View all thumbnails by clicking on the arrows

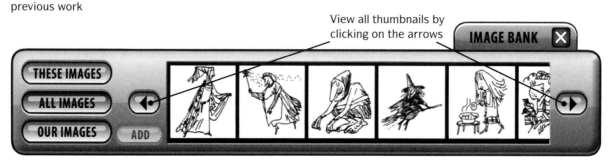

Image bank – click and drag an image to add it to an activity

## Image bank

Each CD-ROM has an 'Image bank' containing images appropriate to the genre being taught. Click on the tab at the bottom right of the screen to open the 'Image bank'. On the left-hand side there are three large buttons.

- The 'These images' button will display only the images associated with the specific activity currently open.
- The 'All images' button will display all the photographs and illustrations available on the CD-ROM.
- The 'Our images' button will contain any images you or the children have added to the CD-ROM.

Press the left or right arrows to scroll through the images available. Select an image and drag and drop it into the desired location on the screen. If necessary, resize the image using the arrow icon that appears at the bottom right of the image.

You can upload images to the 'Image bank', including digital photographs or images drawn and scanned into the computer. Click on 'Our images' and then 'Add' to navigate to where the image is stored. A thumbnail picture will be added to the gallery.

## Writing your own story

Each CD-ROM contains a selection of blank writing templates. The fiction genre templates will be categorised under the button 'My story' and the non-fiction templates will be categorised under 'My recount' or 'My writing'. The writing templates encourage the children to produce an extended piece of genre writing. They can also add images, speech bubbles and use other tools to enhance their work.

The fiction titles also include a cover template for the children to use. They can customise their cover by adding their own title, blurb and images.

# Section 1
# Using good examples

## Poetry features

### Subject
- Themes.
- The natural world.
- Objects in the made world.
- Personal feelings.
- Familiar situations.
- Personal and common experiences.
- Imaginary worlds.
- Senses.

### Structure
- Pattern.
- Shape.
- Forms, such as verses, limericks, couplets and acrostic.

### Rhyme
- Rhyming words and sounds.
- Alliteration.
- Tongue twisters.
- Nonsense words and sounds.
- Repetition.

### Language
- Description.
- Humour.
- Onomatopoeia.
- Use of textual devices such as punctuation, shape and size of lettering.

## Using poetry

Poetry provides a link between the spoken and written word, and between the worlds of reality and imagination. Many Key Stage 1 children are already acquainted with poems through nursery and action rhymes. They enjoy hearing them, saying them and reading them over and over again. Often these well loved verses have led children into the experience of reading and writing. Poems are wonderful for shared and individual reading, providing an accessible introduction to humour in writing and to the possibilities for exploring the imagination. Through shared reading of poetry and the extracts on photocopiable pages 10-13, children can be introduced to key features of the genre.

Draw attention to the sounds of rhymes as you read aloud. Try a 'rhyme challenge' – making up first lines of couplets in the style of 'Catch a Little Rhyme' (Extract 2) and asking the children to provide the second rhyming line. For example: 'I threw it into the sky' (rhymes could be 'fly', 'try', 'cry'); 'I sailed it on the sea' ('free', 'bee', 'me'). This game will highlight the way rhyme works and show how the second line of a couplet continues the sense of the first.

When looking for subjects for poems, ask the children to create rhymes about objects around them, themselves or their friends. Remember that poetry can be as much about wordplay and enjoyment of language, as form and content.

## Poetry and the Primary Framework

The Literacy Framework provides detailed guidance for teaching and learning about poetry at Key Stage 1. In Year 1, the Poetry units focus on: 'Using the senses', 'Pattern and rhyme' and 'Poems on a theme'; in Year 2, the Poetry units focus on: 'Patterns on the page', 'Really looking' and 'Silly stuff'. Children should have access to a wide range of poems and be encouraged to write poems of their own, as enjoying and exploring poetry is a fundamental aspect of children's literacy development. The activities in this book address objectives across the Literacy Framework with greater emphasis on Strands 7–10 ('Understanding and interpreting texts', 'Engaging with and responding to texts', 'Creating and shaping texts', 'Text structure and organisation').

## Extract 1: Ten Green Dragons

### What's on the CD-ROM

**Ten Green Dragons**
- Text extract to read and discuss.

**Satisfying sequences**
- Drag and drop lines to complete each couplet.

The first extract introduces patterned language and rhyme through the familiar form of a counting poem.

- Open the extract 'Ten Green Dragons' from the CD-ROM and read the poem aloud. Identify the repeated words 'In the cave dwelt dragons' and discuss how this builds the poem towards its ending, while aiding an understanding of its content.

- Establish that this is a counting rhyme and explore how the number of dragons decreases gradually as the poem progresses. Did anyone spot the missing number seven? Invent a suitable couplet together so that this number can be included.

- Open 'Satisfying sequences' from the CD-ROM and read the instructions. Ask: *Which sentence will come first if the sequence moves down from five to one? Which sentence will come last?* Drag and drop the children's chosen sentence into the first box and ask them to read the couplet they have created. Continue in this way until all five boxes are filled and the poem is complete.

- Provide each child with a copy of photocopiable page 14 'Satisfying sequences' to complete as instructed.

- Come together to compose a similar counting poem, with the same starting lines linked to different rhymes to form the new couplets.

## Extract 2: Catch a Little Rhyme

### What's on the CD-ROM

**Catch a Little Rhyme**
- Text extract to read and discuss.

**Creating couplets**
- Drag and drop lines to create rhyming couplets.

The second extract introduces children to a nonsense poem arranged in rhyming couplets.

- Display the second extract from the CD-ROM. Read the poem and discuss the title 'Catch a Little Rhyme'. Ask: *Could someone really catch a rhyme? How could it change into all those strange things?* Point out that anything is possible in a nonsense poem.

- Discuss the poem's structure and identify the rhymes. Explain that rhyming couplets are a popular poetic form.

- Open 'Creating couplets' from the CD-ROM. Drag and drop lines into the correct spaces. Read the resulting two lines together and, if the choice does not rhyme satisfactorily, keep trying until everyone is satisfied. Complete all of the couplets in this way.

- Display photocopiable page 15 'Creating couplets'. Ask: *Which words would be suitable to open the poem? Would the opening words from a fairytale, 'Once upon a time', help to indicate that this is a strange, magical poem?* Discuss how the remaining couplets might be linked logically, for example, getting on a bicycle to chase the rhyme after it ran out of the door.

- Provide individual copies for the children to complete.

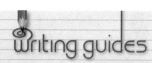

# Extract 3: A Den For All Seasons

## What's on the CD-ROM

**A Den For All Seasons**
- Text extract to read, discuss and edit.

**My secret den**
- Roll over the questions to reveal possible answers.

The third extract can be used to help children to plan and write themed poetry.

- Display 'A Den For All Seasons' from the CD-ROM. Read the poem and discuss the poet's experiences within the den. Point out that four of the verses describe changes from each season. Use the highlighter tool to identify seasonal words.

- Discuss and experiment with ways of editing the extract to improve it. For example, by enhancing description with more effective words, changing letter sizes and fonts to highlight the seasons and so on.

- Open 'My secret den' from the CD-ROM. Explain that this activity will help with planning a poem about a secret den. Read the questions in the first box and roll over the text to reveal ideas. Ask: *Where else might you build a secret den? Will you use rhyme in your poem?* Roll over the remaining questions and continue the discussion.

- Recall the structure of 'A Den For All Seasons' and ask the children how they might structure their poems, for example, with verses about how the den affects different senses.

- Hand out photocopiable page 16 'My secret den' and ask the children to plan a poem entitled 'My secret den'.

- Come together to listen to and discuss the children's poems.

# Poster: Recipe for a poem

## What's on the CD-ROM

**Recipe for a poem**
- Roll over the recipe to reveal suitable words relating to key features.

The poster encourages children to recall previous activities and discussions when writing poetry.

- Display the 'Recipe for a poem' poster from the CD-ROM. Explore the information, or 'ingredients', relating to the key features of a poem. Explain that, when following a recipe, you need to find the right ingredients and mix them carefully to make something good. It's the same with a poem. Relate the 'ingredients' displayed on the poster to the poems on pages 10–13, noting they are not all used in each.

- Roll over the sections of the recipe to reveal in the cauldron further text depicting examples of words related to the ingredients, such as rhyming and descriptive words.

- Provide photocopiable page 18 'Recipe for a poem' for children to refer to, or enlarge it to display as a class prompt sheet. Explore a few poems and ask the children to work out their own ingredients, with reference to the poster. This will build their understanding of verse and provide different examples to think about when writing their own poetry in Sections 2 and 3.

- Ask the children to discuss their favourite poems and hand out photocopiable page 17 'My favourite poem' for them to complete.

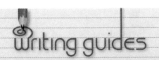

# Extract 1: Ten Green Dragons

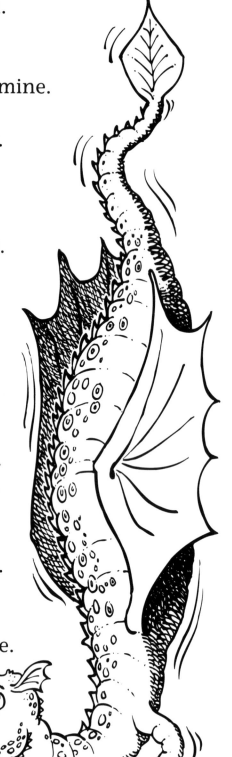

In the cave dwelt dragons ten.
One fell fighting four horsemen.

In the cave dwelt dragons nine.
One went down the deep, dark mine.

In the cave dwelt dragons eight.
Two forgot to hibernate.

In the cave dwelt dragons six.
One dropped dead from politics.

In the cave dwelt dragons five.
One took a dive in overdrive.

In the cave dwelt dragons four.
One got struck by a meteor.

In the cave dwelt dragons three.
One ran off with a chimpanzee.

In the cave dwelt dragons two.
One went onto the King's menu.

In the cave dwelt dragons one.
Laid ten eggs and then was gone.

*Nick Toczek*

*Text © 1997, Nick Toczek; illustration © 2003, Mary Hall.*

Writing guides

# Extract 2: Catch a Little Rhyme

Once upon a time
I caught a little rhyme

I set it on the floor
but it ran out the door

I chased it on my bicycle
but it melted to an icicle

I scooped it up in my hat
but it turned into a cat

I caught it by the tail
but it stretched into a whale

I followed it in a boat
but it changed into a goat

When I fed it tin and paper
it became a tall skyscraper

Then it grew into a kite
and flew far out of sight...

*Eve Merriam*

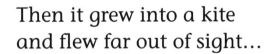

*Text © 1966, Eve Merriam; illustration © 2003, Mary Hall.*

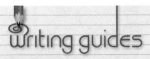

# Extract 3: A Den For All Seasons

I have a dark and secret den,
Hidden high in a leafy tree,
Where it's safe and warm and cosy,
And there's only just room for me.

In spring I like to sit and stare,
As birds nest and blossom flowers,
While rich new leaves give me shelter,
From the sudden April showers.

In autumn I just lie and dream,
Relaxed from my head to my toes,
The winds fan my hair and rock me,
While the dead leaves tickle my nose.

In summer I wear camouflage,
Shadowed cow prints of black and white,
Painted by leaves that fan and cool,
As they let in the sun's bright light.

In winter I'm wisely grounded,
A secret den is not for me,
When snow falls on icy branches,
It's then that I go home for tea!

*Jean Evans*

*Illustration © 2010, Mike Phillips/Beehive Illustration.*

# Satisfying sequences

● Cut out the five sentences at the bottom of the sheet and match each of them to one of the top five sentences to make rhyming pairs.

> **In the cave dwelt dragons five.**

> **In the cave dwelt dragons four.**

> **In the cave dwelt dragons three.**

> **In the cave dwelt dragons two.**

> **In the cave dwelt dragons one.**

| One went onto the King's menu. |
| One got struck by a meteor. |
| Laid ten eggs and then was gone. |
| One took a dive in overdrive. |
| One ran off with a chimpanzee. |

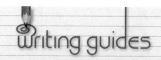

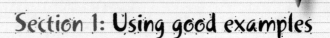
# Creating couplets

● Cut out the lines of text and put them into pairs to create rhyming pairs.

● Rearrange the pairs into the best order to complete your poem.

| | |
|---|---|
| I caught it by the tail | but it turned into a cat |
| I followed it in a boat | it became a tall skyscraper |
| I set it on the floor | but it changed into a goat |
| Then it grew into a kite | I caught a little rhyme |
| I chased it on my bicycle | and flew far out of sight... |
| Once upon a time | but it ran out the door |
| When I fed it tin and paper | but it melted to an icicle |
| I scooped it up in my hat | but it stretched into a whale |

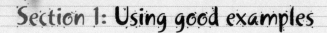
## Section 1: Using good examples

# My secret den

- Create a poem about a secret den.
- Use the questions below to help you plan your poem, think of describing words. If you are using rhyming words include them below.

| Where have you made your den? |
| --- |
| What is the inside of your den like? |
| What can you see from your den? |
| When would you visit your den? |
| How does your den feel and smell? |
| What would you put in your den? |

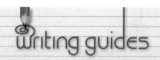
writing guides

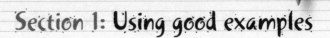

# My favourite poem

● Review your favourite poem by completing each of the sections below.

● Write your own sentences in the bottom box.

---

The title of the poem is: _____

The poem is written by: _____

---

### The subject

The poem is about: _____

Is the subject of the poem real?          Yes ⬜ No ⬜

Is the subject of the poem imaginary?     Yes ⬜ No ⬜

---

### The structure

Is the poem written in verses?            Yes ⬜ No ⬜

Is the poem written in rhyming pairs?     Yes ⬜ No ⬜

Does the poem have rhyming words
at the end of each line?                  Yes ⬜ No ⬜

---

### The language

Does the poem have lots of describing words?  Yes ⬜ No ⬜

Does the poem have some nonsense words?       Yes ⬜ No ⬜

Is the poem easy to read and understand?      Yes ⬜ No ⬜

---

Write some sentences about why you like the poem.

_____

_____

_____

---

# Recipe for a poem

## 1. Subject
Choose a subject that is interesting or funny and gives you a good feeling.

## 2. Structure
Prepare a good structure.

## 3. Rhyme
Perhaps add a spoonful of rhymes.

## 4. Language
Add a big handful of describing words. Perhaps add some nonsense.

## 5. Mix
Put them all into a big pot of ideas and stir with your pencil.

## 6. Compose
Out comes a delightful poem!

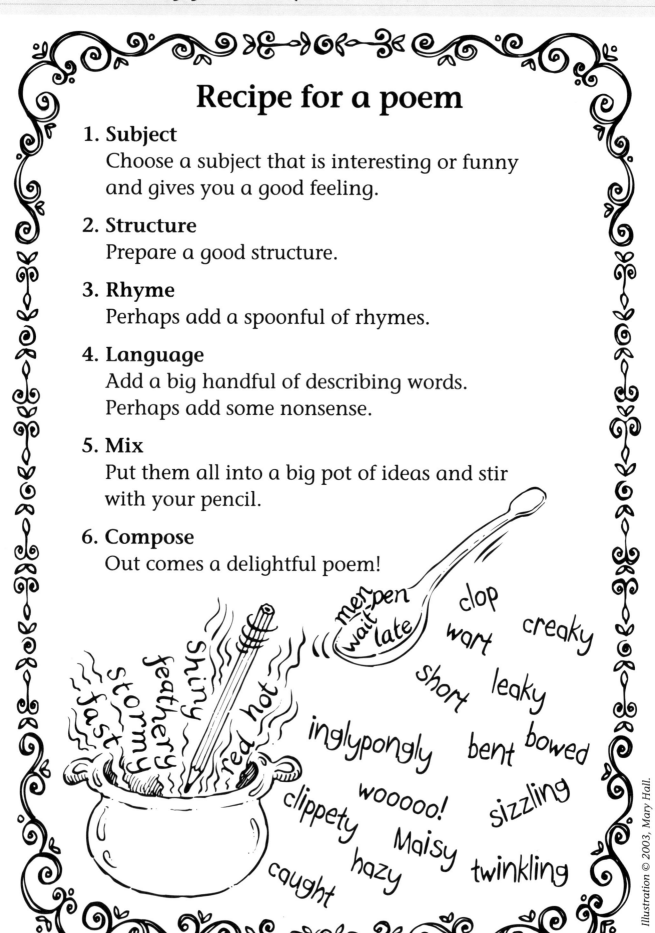

men pen wait late clop wart creaky short leaky inglypongly bent bowed wooooo! sizzling clippety Maisy twinkling hazy caught shiny feathery stormy fast red hot

Illustration © 2003, Mary Hall.

writing guides

# Section 2
# Developing writing

The activities in this section provide opportunities for children to appreciate the wealth and richness of poetry, from thought-provoking descriptive verse to rollicking humour. There are exciting opportunities to explore the key elements of poetry. These include:

- Subject: the children are encouraged to compose poems that reflect their personal feelings relating to familiar topics. The CD-ROM resources will enrich children's use of vocabulary and provide opportunities to use imaginative language.

- Structure: these activities will encourage children to explore structure and pattern in poetry by focusing on limericks and shape poems.

- Rhyme: the children explore the satisfying effect of alliteration in poetry, with the added enjoyment of trying out some tongue twisters. Nonsense poems are included so that children can write about weird and exciting creatures.

- Language: poems introduce children to a wealth of rich, diverse and humorous language not usually encountered during day-to-day life. The importance of humour in poetry is investigated and children are encouraged to explore and write about funny situations and nonsense worlds.

## How to use the activities

Detailed teachers' notes give guidance on delivery, including how to support each activity using the photocopiable sheets at the end of the section and the materials on the CD-ROM. Children are encouraged to employ a range of strategies to create their poetry, and a variety of simple writing templates are provided to support the development of their independent writing. Through discussion activities, dramatisation, poetry reading and reciting, children can review and modify their ideas before writing them down. The activities are flexible and can easily be adapted. They should be modelled to the class or smaller groups using the whiteboard before the children undertake independent work. The children's on-screen work and completed photocopiable sheets can be saved to form a resource bank of ideas for use in their poetry writing.

## Activities breakdown

### Subject
- Weather words (page 20)
- Seasonal settings (page 20)
- Poetic pets and places (page 21)

### Structure
- Shaping a robot poem (page 21)
- Lively limericks (page 22)

### Rhyme
- Tripping off the tongue (page 22)
- Nonsense poems (page 23)

### Language
- What is it like? (page 23)
- Just imagine! (page 24)
- Using my senses (page 24)

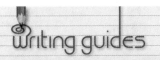

# Activity 1: Weather words

## Objective

To spell with increasing accuracy and confidence, drawing on word recognition and knowledge of word structure, and spelling patterns.
(Year 2 Strand 5)

## What's on the CD-ROM

**Weather words**
- Roll over boxes to reveal rhyming weather words.

**Media resources**
- Display and discuss the 'Snow' image.
- Listen to and discuss the 'Wind' audio clip.

## What to do

This activity encourages children to consider weather-related rhyming words and highlights alternative ways of spelling common phonemes.

- Ask the children to recall traditional weather poems, such as 'I Hear Thunder', 'The North Wind Doth Blow' and 'Rain, Rain Go Away'. Identify the rhyming words in each example.

- Open 'Weather words' from the CD-ROM. Ask individuals to roll over each box to reveal hidden words. Read the words together and notice the spelling and how they rhyme. Discuss how they might link to the weather condition in a poem.

- Display the snow photograph and together recall snow-related rhyming words from the roll over text. Invite suggestions for additional non-rhyming snow-related words to add to them.

- Listen to the audio clip of the wind before writing wind-related rhyming words on the board, such as 'howl', 'growl', 'wail' and 'gale'.

- Provide each child with photocopiable page 25 'Weather words' and ask them to complete it, recalling the class discussion.

- Bring the class together so the children can read their weather verses aloud. Invite constructive comments on the suitability of chosen words.

# Activity 2: Seasonal settings

## Objective

To group written sentences together in chunks of meaning or subjects.
(Year 1 Strand 10)

## What's on the CD-ROM

**A Den For All Seasons**
- Poem to discuss.

**Media resources**
- Discuss the 'Autumn tree' and 'Snow' images.

**Seasonal settings**
- Drag and drop words to the correct season.
- Type in seasonal words.

## What to do

This activity will enhance children's ability to choose appropriate words for poems linked to a given subject and compose verses with a specific focus.

- Display and read 'A Den For All Seasons' from the CD-ROM. Discuss how each season is identified in a separate verse. Ask the children to point to words that link each verse to a season, for example, 'bird's nest' and 'icy branches'.

- Display the 'Autumn tree' and 'Snow' images and invite the children to identify the seasons. Use exciting words to describe them, such as 'multicoloured autumn leaves' or 'sparkling winter snow'.

- Open 'Seasonal settings' from the CD-ROM. Choose children to drag and drop words into the correct 'season' boxes and then to type in their own words.

- Provide each child with an A3 copy of photocopiable page 26 'Seasonal settings' to complete. Then encourage them as a class to discuss the range of words used.

- Using their activity notes ask the children to write their own poems entitled 'Seasons'.

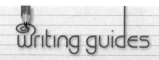

# Activity 3: Poetic pets and places

## Objective

To independently choose what to write about, plan and follow it through. (Year 1 Strand 9)

### What to do

This activity stimulates children's imaginations prior to writing a fantasy poem.

● Read aloud 'On Holiday with Grandma' by Robin Mellor, or another suitable poem that does not rhyme.

● Talk about how poems can still be effective when they have no regular rhyming structure.

● Ask why this poem is funny and discuss the unexpected things that Grandma does. Do the children ever get into mischief? Perhaps they have a pet that is prone to pranks?

● Display an enlarged version of photocopiable page 27 'Poetic pets and places' and read it together. Discuss unexpected things that pets might do in the places illustrated. Give examples of verbs and descriptive words to reinforce an understanding of instructions.

● Provide each child with the photocopiable sheet to complete.

● Bring the class together to share their poems.

# Activity 4: Shaping a robot poem

## Objective

To select from different presentational features to suit particular writing purposes on paper and on screen. (Year 2 Strand 9)

## What's on the CD-ROM

**Media resources**
● Display and discuss the 'Skyscraper' image.

**A Den For All Seasons**
● Discuss the presentation of the poem.

**Shaping a robot poem**
● Roll over the robot to reveal rhyming phrases.

### What to do

This activity encourages children to explore the effectiveness of creating visual shapes with words.

● Display the image of the skyscraper from the CD-ROM and discuss the shape of the building. Together think of rhyming words related to a skyscraper, for example, 'high', 'sky', 'tall', 'wall', 'busy' and 'dizzy'. Write them in the centre of the board, as a list, to create a tall thin skyscraper-shaped poem.

● Open 'A Den For All Seasons' from the CD-ROM. Discuss how the poem is visually presented, for example, where the verses are positioned. Talk about whether this layout enhances the overall effectiveness of the poem.

● Open 'Shaping a robot poem' from the CD-ROM and roll over the robot to reveal rhyming phrases related to body parts.

● Arrange the children in groups and supply each group with a copy of photocopiable page 28 'Shaping a robot poem'. Read the instructions and ask them to complete this plan and then write a robot poem in their small groups. They will need to choose a scribe and someone to read the finished poem to the class.

● Bring the class together to discuss the effectiveness of their poems.

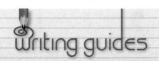

# Activity 5: Lively limericks

## Objective

To explain their reactions to texts, commenting on important aspects. (Year 2 Strand 8)

## What's on the CD-ROM

**Lively limericks**
- Roll over text to reveal rhyming words for character and place names.
- Type in a chosen character and place.
- Compose and type in a complete limerick.

### What to do

This activity explores the structure of limericks and encourages children to compose their own.

- Read some of Edward Lear's limericks to the class. For example, 'There was a young lady whose bonnet' and 'There was an old lady whose folly'.

- Explore a few typical limericks in more detail together. Point out the limerick rhyming structure AABBA. Explain that lines one, two and five generally have seven to ten syllables and lines three and four have five to seven. Count them to check.

- Open 'Lively limericks' from the CD-ROM and roll over the text to reveal suitable rhyming words for character names and places.

- Together choose a limerick character name and place. Type them into the indicated spaces.

- Discuss possible limericks around the chosen character or place. Experiment by typing in the children's five lines to form a limerick. Delete and try different options until everyone agrees on a version.

- Provide each child with photocopiable page 29 'Lively limericks' to complete independently.

- Encourage the class to share limericks and constructive comments.

# Activity 6: Tripping off the tongue

## Objective

To explore the effect of patterns of language and repeated words and phrases. (Year 1 Strand 7)

## What's on the CD-ROM

**Media resources**
- Display the 'Bonfire' image to stimulate word choices.

### What to do

This activity explores the effect of alliteration in poetry.

- Invite the children to repeat tongue twisters, such as 'Peter Piper' and 'She Sells Seashells'. Discuss why these sentences are called tongue twisters. Do the children tie their tongues in knots by repeating 'Red leather, yellow leather'? Can they identify repeated sounds?

- Display the image of the bonfire from the CD-ROM and create alliterative strings of words to describe it. For example, 'smoky', 'smelly' and 'smouldering'; or 'flashes', 'flames' and 'flares'.

- Display an enlarged version of photocopiable page 30 'Tripping off the tongue'. Read the partially completed sentences and identify the repeated initial sound. Invite the children to choose a word from the selection to complete each sentence. Try the two alternatives.

- As a class invent funny alliterative sentences about the children. For example, 'Frowning Freddy frightened a frog'.

- Hand out the photocopiable sheet for the children to complete.

- Bring the class together to discuss the effectiveness of their choices.

# Activity 7: Nonsense poems

## Objective

To speak with clarity and use appropriate intonation when reading and reciting texts. (Year 2 Strand 1)

## What's on the CD-ROM

**Catch a Little Rhyme**
- A nonsense poem to discuss.

## What to do

This activity explores nonsense poetry and encourages children to compose their own poems.

- Display the extract 'Catch a Little Rhyme' from the CD-ROM. Read this and other nonsense rhymes, such as 'The Jumblies' by Edward Lear and 'On the Ning Nang Nong' by Spike Milligan. Discuss why these rhymes fall into the category of nonsense poetry.

- Display an enlarged version of photocopiable page 31 'Nonsense poems' and explain how it will help them compose a nonsense poem.

- Explore the image of a dog and ask how the children might transform this ordinary animal into a nonsense character, for example, by giving it three heads and the body of a fish. Repeat with the image of an ordinary collar and lead, considering what nonsense item might be used by the new character, such as a fish tank on wheels.

- Provide each child with a copy of the photocopiable sheet to complete. Read out the instructions to ensure they understand what to do. Once they have finished, ask them to write their own nonsense poem.

- Bring the class together to read their poems aloud, emphasising nonsense aspects for greater effect.

# Activity 8: What is it like?

## Objective

To listen to others in class, ask relevant questions and follow instructions. (Year 2 Strand 2)

## What to do

This activity encourages children to choose appropriate words to describe objects and ask relevant questions to determine the subject of poems.

- Display an enlarged version of photocopiable page 32 'What is it like?' and ask the class to suggest interesting words to describe the objects. For example, the elephant can be described as 'massive', 'huge' or 'gigantic' (not just 'big'). Invite them to select their own object.

- Highlight the last part of the sheet and read out this example of a short verse that starts to use describing words to fit into a poetic pattern.

> One, two, three,
> What can I see?
> The bright golden sun,
> And it's shining down on me.

- Provide each child with the photocopiable sheet to complete.

- Once the children have finished, organise them to work in small groups. Invite the children to ask each other questions about the subject of their poems and then to guess. For example: *Is it alive? Can I eat it?*

- Bring the class together to discuss words used and decide which questions proved most relevant.

# Activity 9: Just imagine!

## Objective

To explain their views to others in a small group, decide how to report the group's views to the class. (Year 1 Strand 3)

## What to do

Invite children to use their imagination to explore nonsense worlds.

- Explain to the children that nonsense verse can take us into strange, unknown worlds. Read examples of rhyming text in books about nonsense worlds, for example, *Here Come the Aliens!* by Colin McNaughton (Walker books).

- Discuss the meaning of 'topsy turvy'. Ask the children to imagine what a topsy-turvy world would be like. Ask: *When would you wake up? Where would you wear your socks?*

- Emphasise that the poems the children are going to create do not have to rhyme, as strange ideas are the most important element. Create a poem together set in a nonsense world. Write your ideas on the board. Make sure that all events are opposite to normal.

- Working in groups, hand out photocopiable page 33 'Just imagine!'. Ask them to use some or all of the pictures on the sheet as subjects or settings for a nonsense poem entitled 'Just imagine!'. Emphasise the importance of planning the structure before writing.

- Bring the class together to share and discuss their poems.

# Activity 10: Using my senses

## Objective

To compose and write simple sentences independently to communicate meaning. (Year 1 Strand 11)

## What's on the CD-ROM

### Media resources
- Listen to the 'Wind' audio clip.
- Explore the 'Bonfire' and 'Snow' images.

### Using my senses
- Roll over the questions to reveal answers.
- Drag and drop words to the correct question.

## What to do

This activity encourages children to identify how they use their senses before writing poems about them.

- Listen to the audio clip of wind whistling. How does this sound make the children feel? Does it remind them of any past experiences?

- Display the image of the bonfire from the CD-ROM and ask the children to consider how a bonfire looks, smells and sounds. Do the same with the image of snow, also discussing how snow feels and tastes.

- Open 'Using my senses' from the CD-ROM. Read each question and roll over them to reveal possible answers. Drag and drop the words from the bottom of the screen to the correct question boxes.

- Display an enlarged version of photocopiable page 34 'Using my senses'. Discuss the purpose of the body parts in the left-hand boxes. Read the questions in the right-hand boxes and invite the children to think of things that each body part can do, for example, ears can hear music.

- Provide each child with a copy of the sheet to complete.

- Invite the children to use their completed sheets and memories of earlier discussions to help them to write a poem based around the five senses.

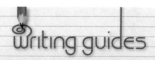
writing guides

# Weather words

- Write some rhyming words for each type of weather.

 **sun**

fun

 **rain**

lane

 **snow**

go

 **wet**

yet

 **cold**

old

 **sleet**

feet

- Choose two types of weather to write verses about.
Make sure you put your rhyming words in the right place.

I like _____

_____

I like _____

_____

# Seasonal settings

- Cut out the words at the bottom of the sheet and stick them into the correct season boxes.
- Add some words of your own to each box.

**Summer**

My summer words…

**Winter**

My winter words…

**Spring**

My spring words…

**Autumn**

My autumn words…

| snow | sunshine | lambs | conkers | ice | picnics | falling leaves | blossom |
|------|----------|-------|---------|-----|---------|----------------|---------|

*Illustrations © 2010, Mike Phillips/Beehive Illustration.*

writing guides

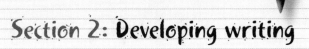

# Poetic pets and places

- Which pet would you like to take out? Circle one.

puppy    kitten    pony    tortoise    spider    goldfish    snake

- Here are some places to take your pet. What might your animal do in each location? Note down some verbs and descriptive words to use.

 school

 library

 playground

 shops

- Use your notes to write a short poem about your poetic pet.

When I took _____

It _____

_____

_____

*Illustrations © 2003, Mary Hall.*

# Shaping a robot poem

● Write notes in the boxes to create a plan to help shape your robot poem.

● Using your notes, on a separate sheet draw and label a picture of your robot, identifying the main sections, 'head', 'body', 'arms' and 'legs'. Then write your robot poem.

---

The first section of my poem will be inside the robot's

_____

Some of the words I will use are:

_____

---

The second section of my poem will be inside the robot's

_____

Some of the words I will use are:

_____

---

The third section of my poem will be inside the robot's

_____

Some of the words I will use are:

_____

---

The fourth section of my poem will be inside the robot's

_____

Some of the words I will use are:

_____

---

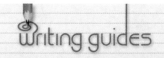

# Lively limericks

● Follow the instructions below to help create your own limerick.

1. Add more rhyming words to the lists after these names.

Pete – meat, beat, greet, feet, heat, _____

Mark – dark, bark, stark, _____

2. Add some rhyming words to continue the lists after these places.

Wales – snails, tales, rails, gales, _____

Poole – cool, rule, school, fool, _____

3. Think of names for limerick characters and places to finish these first lines.

There was an old lady called _____

There was a young boy from _____

4. Write your own limerick in this box.

_____

_____

_____

_____

_____

## Section 2: Developing writing

# Tripping off the tongue

● Complete these sentences using a word from the box below that has the same sound.

Horrid Harry had a huge hairy _____

Mighty Miah made a magnificent _____

Tricky Tracy tied tape to her _____

Cheerful Charlie chewed some _____

Lovely Lucy loved licking _____

| hedgehog | teacher | lollipops | mess | chocolate |
|---|---|---|---|---|
| model | chickweed | limpets | toes | hand |

● Make up funny sentences with the same sounds about two of your friends.

1. _____

_____

2. _____

_____

● Choose words from the bottom box to complete these tongue twisters.

Peter Piper picked a _____ of pickled _____.

She sells sea _____ on the _____ shore.

A noisy _____ annoys a _____ oyster.

| peck | sea | noisy | pepper | shells | noise |
|---|---|---|---|---|---|

# Nonsense poems

● Draw pictures of your nonsense character and object in the empty boxes below. Then complete the sentences.

| Ordinary animal | My nonsense animal |
|---|---|
|  |  |
| Ordinary object for an ordinary animal | A nonsense object for my nonsense animal |
|  |  |

My nonsense character is called a _____

My character is nonsense because it _____

The nonsense object my character has is a _____

My character does this with the nonsense object _____

_____

*Illustrations © 2010, Mike Phillips/Beehive Illustration.*

## Section 2: Developing writing

# What is it like?

● Write some words to describe each picture. Then, in the last box, draw your own object and describe it.

● Choose one picture and use the words in this poem:

One, two, three
What can I see?

The _____

And it's _____ at me.

*Illustrations © 2003, Mary Hall.*

# Just imagine!

● Look at the pictures and try to imagine each object in a nonsense world. What would it be like? What would it do? What would happen? Note your ideas beneath the pictures.

● Use your ideas to write a short nonsense poem.
Start with **Just imagine…**

*Illustrations © 2003, Mary Hall.*

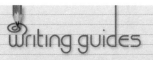 **writing guides**

# Using my senses

● Draw a picture of the part of the body named in each left-hand box.

● Answer the questions in the right-hand boxes – the words at the bottom might help you. Add more words of your own to each box.

| You use your **ears** to hear things. | ➤ | What can you hear? |
|---|---|---|

| You use your **eyes** to see things. | ➤ | What can you see? |
|---|---|---|

| You use your **nose** to smell things. | ➤ | What can you smell? |
|---|---|---|

| You use your **tongue** to taste things. | ➤ | What can you taste? |
|---|---|---|

| You use your **hands** to feel things. | ➤ | What can you feel? |
|---|---|---|

biscuits    carrots    crisps    flowers    food
smoke    people    objects    birds    animals
traffic    talking    laughing

# Section 3

# Writing

After reading, discussing and sharing examples of poetry, and working through the activities in Section 2, children should be aware of key features for this genre and be ready to begin writing their own poems.

The three writing projects in this section provide opportunities to plan and write poems, and the accompanying activities will stimulate the development of various aspects of their poetry writing skills, such as choosing appropriate form, visual presentation and language.

Flexibility is of paramount importance when allocating time for each project, as children will need to progress from their initial ideas to the finished poems at their own pace. They may need several extended writing sessions to plan, draft, redraft and 'publish' their poems. How many will depend on individuals. Some will happily revisit their developing work over several sessions, while others will find returning to unfinished work much more difficult. These children will need to be given extra time and support until they develop the skills needed to restart or redraft their work with confidence.

## Planning the sessions

The three writing projects in this section all progress along a similar format, providing children with the following opportunities:

- Oral sessions to discuss and rehearse ideas in pairs, small groups and as a whole class.

- Shared sessions to use planning frames to convert shared ideas into written poems using the 'My poem' writing templates on the CD-ROM.

- Independent sessions to work alone, repeating the work undertaken in the shared session, planning and writing individual poems. These can be presented on screen using the 'My poem' writing templates or on paper as extended writing.

## Providing support

Ensure that appropriate support is given to individuals throughout the whole writing process. Refer the children to the poster on photocopiable page 18 'Recipe for a poem' or revisit the interactive version for further ideas when planning and drafting their poetry. Recall particular activities from previous sessions to support specific aspects, for example, using different visual presentations for a poem ('Shaping a robot poem' page 21) or exploring a particular theme ('Seasonal settings' page 20).

As well as providing examples of different types of poetry, motivate the children by introducing a range of formats for presenting work. For example, individual computers, books, paper of different colours and sizes, decorative borders and so on.

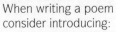

## Writing tips

When writing a poem consider introducing:
- unusual characters
- interesting themes
- regular verse structure
- patterned language and repetition
- alliteration and tongue twisters
- nonsense words and sounds
- acrostic verse (when certain letters spell out another word)
- rhyming couplets
- describing words
- punctuation, such as exclamation marks
- presentation techniques, such as varying font and letter sizes, and images.

# Project 1: Looking out of the window

## Objectives

To independently choose what to write about, plan and follow it through.
(Year 1 Strand 9)
To use planning to establish clear sections for writing.
(Year 2 Strand 10)

## What's on the CD-ROM

**Looking out of the window**
- Roll over each bubble to reveal a poet's thoughts.

**Poem planner**
- Complete the poem planning frame.

**My poem**
- Compose a poem using the writing templates.

## What to do

This activity stimulates children's imaginations and teaches them how to write a poem using the planning and writing templates on the CD-ROM.

- Open 'Looking out of the window' from the CD-ROM and explain that the girl pictured is writing poems about what she can see out of the window. Roll over the thought bubbles to reveal the girl's thoughts. Distinguish between words that describe real and imagined things in the second and third pictures.

- Open 'Poem planner' from the CD-ROM (by clicking on the 'Planning' button in the main menu). Complete the sections of the planner together. Refer to the previous discussion about real and imaginary subjects and discuss poems encountered or invented by the children for inspiration. Type in agreed responses to questions about the chosen poem type, subject and structure, and provide examples of the language and presentation to be included. This plan will help form the class poem.

- Open 'My poem' from the CD-ROM and choose one of the writing templates to open a page. Explain that the children can present a whole poem on this page or add additional pages if the poem is longer. Show them how to drag and drop an appropriate image from the 'Image bank' onto the page and demonstrate how to resize it. (It is possible to upload extra images into the 'Image bank' if children wish to.) Type the first line of the class poem into a suitably positioned box, modifying and editing until the children are satisfied.

- Type in the remainder of the class poem, arranging verses or lines to fit the chosen template. If necessary, open another page (template) by clicking on 'Add page'. Continue in the same way by selecting page layouts, choosing images, orally drafting and finally writing text.

- Explore the tools available to enhance presentation, for example, changing letter size and font.

- Read the finished poem together and discuss content and presentation. Make modifications until everyone is satisfied with the creation.

- Provide each child with photocopiable page 38 'Looking out of the window' to complete, this will help them focus on the detail and language in their own poems.

- Display and hand out photocopiable page 39 'Real or imagined?'. Explain that each scene the children draw and describe will provide inspiration for their poetry writing.

- Give each child photocopiable page 43 'Poem planner' and invite them to plan a poem based on their ideas generated from photocopiable pages 38 and 39.

- Ask the children to use the 'My poem' writing templates to compose their own poems.

 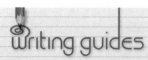

# Project 2: Out and about

## Objective

To create short simple texts on paper and screen that combine words with images (and sounds). (Year 1 Strand 9)

## What's on the CD-ROM

**Out and about**
● Drag and drop words to the correct landscape.

**Poem planner**
● Complete the poem planning frame.

**My poem**
● Compose a poem using the writing templates.

## What to do

This activity reinforces poetry writing skills by asking children to compose poems about the outdoors.

● Discuss what the children like and dislike about outdoor landscapes. Open 'Out and about' from the CD-ROM and compare the four landscapes depicted. Read the words at the bottom of the screen and decide which of the landscapes to drag and drop them into.

● Display an enlarged version of photocopiable page 41 'The tree of rhyme'. Ask the class to think of rhyming words for those on the sheet. Make connections between the words and the landscapes explored.

● Provide each child with photocopiable pages 40 and 41, 'Out and about' and 'The tree of rhyme'. Suggest that the children discuss their ideas in pairs initially, referring to the on-screen activity if required.

● Bring the children together and open the 'Poem planner' from the CD-ROM. Create a shared plan for a poem about the outdoors.

● Open 'My poem' from the CD-ROM (see Project 1 for instructions of how to use). Write the planned poem together.

● Ask the children to plan and write their own poem about the outdoors using 'Poem planner' and 'My poem' on the CD-ROM.

# Project 3: Picking the right words

## Objective

To make adventurous word and language choices appropriate to the style and purpose of the text. (Year 2 Strand 9)

## What's on the CD-ROM

**Poem planner**
● Complete the poem planning frame.

**My poem**
● Compose a poem using the writing templates.

## What to do

This activity allows the children to focus on the language used in poems.

● Display an enlarged version of photocopiable page 42 'Picking the right words'. Explain that, although all of the words in each flower mean approximately the same thing, some can be more effective than others depending on how and where they are used. Choose two of these words at random and think of something they might describe, for example, 'shiny' and 'squelchy' would describe wet clay more effectively than 'glittering'.

● Hand out photocopiable page 42 and invite the children to complete the flowers by suggesting appropriate words for each empty petal.

● Ask the children to compose a poem using some or all of the words in one of the flowers. Suggest an example, such as:

> The bright sun was so hot,
> Sizzling onto my skin,
> I felt as if I was really boiling!
> What a scorching summer's day.

● Encourage the children to plan and write their poem as a piece of extended writing, using the 'Poem planner' (photocopiable page 43) and 'My poem' writing templates on the CD-ROM.

# Looking out of the window

● Before writing a poem, a poet thinks very hard and gets ready to use attractive words and great ideas.

● What do you think the girl is thinking about in each picture? Write some words inside each thought bubble.

Try looking out of the window. Remember a poet can see something **real**…

…or something amazing they have **imagined**.

writing guides

# Real or imagined?

● Different poets see different things. Imagine what you might see through these windows.

● Draw a real scene and an imaginary scene. Write some words to describe the scene at the sides of each one.

**Real**

**Imagined**

● Write down a title for a poem you might write after looking at the view from each window.

Real: _____

Imagined: _____

Illustrations © 2003, Mary Hall.

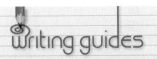

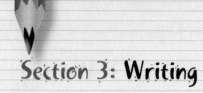
# Out and about

● Read the words in the bottom box and decide which of the pictured landscapes they might be found in. Write them under your chosen landscape.

A busy city

The countryside

Mountains

The seaside

*Illustrations © 2010, Mike Phillips/Beehive Illustration.*

| snow | farms | buildings | shells | lanes | traffic |
| climbers | fields | waves | steep | people | boats |

# The tree of rhyme

● Add as many rhyming words as you can.

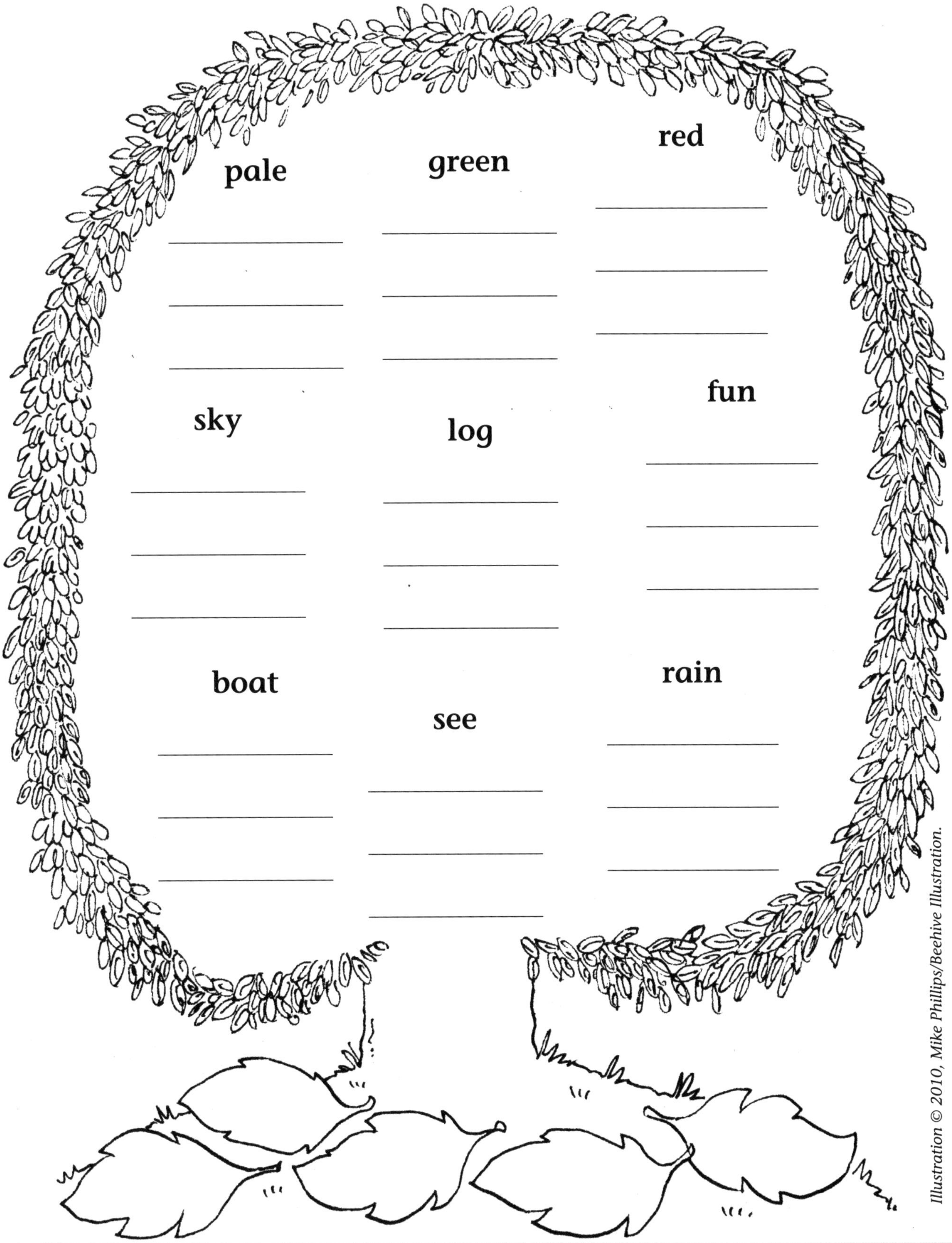

**pale**

_____

_____

_____

**green**

_____

_____

_____

**red**

_____

_____

_____

**sky**

_____

_____

_____

**log**

_____

_____

_____

**fun**

_____

_____

_____

**boat**

_____

_____

_____

**see**

_____

_____

_____

**rain**

_____

_____

_____

_Illustration © 2010, Mike Phillips/Beehive Illustration._

# Picking the right words

● Can you think of more words that would fit into the flowers?

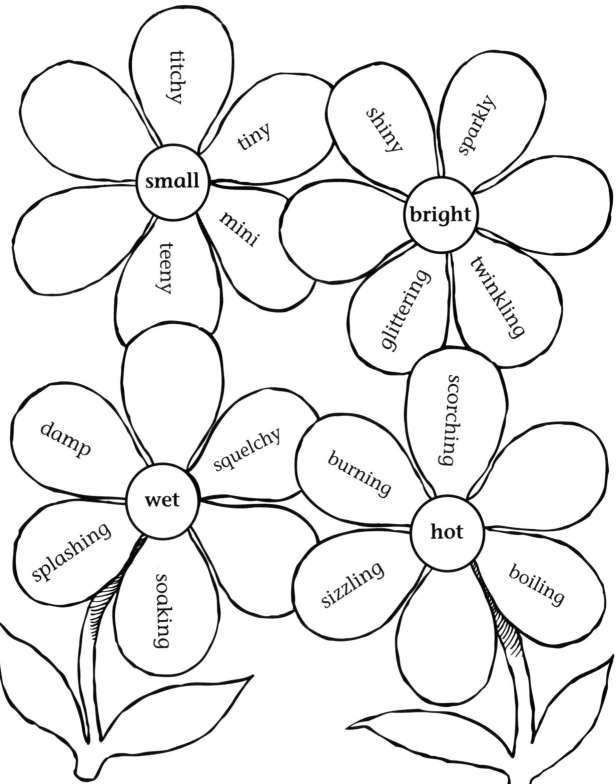

small — titchy, tiny, mini, teeny

bright — shiny, sparkly, glittering, twinkling

wet — damp, squelchy, splashing, soaking

hot — scorching, burning, sizzling, boiling

● Choose one flower. Write a poem using these words.

# Poem planner

● Use this page to plan your own poem.

**Type**
What type of poem do you plan to write?

Who do you think will enjoy your poem?

**Subject**
What is your poem about?

Is the subject real or imaginary?

**Structure**
Describe what form your poem will take.

**Language**
Write down some of the words you plan to use.

**Presentation**
Write down any special features you plan to use.

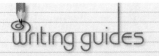

# Section 4

# Review

Regularly reviewing the children's poems is vital in helping you to appreciate how effectively they have used all they have learned, from understanding that poetry can take many forms but is different from other writing forms, to the world of imagination that a poet can explore. Through ongoing assessment, individual progress towards specific learning targets can be monitored and the next steps for learning planned at the child's own level. Equally relevant is the reviewing of overall progress at the end of a unit of work, to identify areas of teaching and learning that need to be reinforced or modified. Gaps in learning can be addressed by revisiting the relevant lesson section.

## Self review

Children should be encouraged to engage in an ongoing process of self review. Encourage them to look constantly at their work and ask themselves questions about it. Try to instil a desire for improving a poem; for changing it to make it sound and look better. Photocopiable page 45 'Self review' has been designed to be used by children independently in order to decide how successful they have been in introducing features of the poetry genre into their own writing. Demonstrate how to use the page initially to review a poem that you have created together.

## Peer review

Sharing a poem with a partner is a positive and useful reviewing method. Discuss the children's roles as writing partners beforehand to ensure that the comments given are constructive and supportive. Photocopiable page 46 'Peer review' involves working with writing partners of a similar ability to motivate children into reviewing and redrafting their written work. Explain to the children that they should answer the questions on the photocopiable sheet. This will enable their partners to gain feedback on how well their poems engage the reader and/or listener.

## Teacher review

The assessment of the children's poems should focus on their use of key features of poetry explored in the previous sections. However, you can also look for evidence that the children understand different forms of poetry, such as couplets, limericks and nonsense verse.

The grid on photocopiable page 47 'Teacher review' has been designed to enable you to assess evidence of children's progress and attainment at the end of a unit of work on poems. It is linked to the National Curriculum's eight Assessment Focus objectives for writing.

As you consider children's work in relation to each Assessment Focus, it is essential to look at different types of evidence, for example, the language children use or their ability to create a recognisable form.

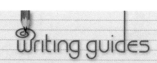

Section 4: Review

# Self review

● Read your poem and complete the sections below.

| |
|---|
| Title of poem: |
| My poem was about |
| I used these describing words: |
| My poem was in this form: |
| The most difficult part of writing my poem was |
| The part of my poem I like the best is |

*Illustration © 2003, Mary Hall.*

# Peer review

● Read your partner's poem and complete the sections below.

| |
|---|
| Title of poem: |
| Written by: |
| This poem was about |
| My favourite word (say why) is: |
| My favourite phrase (say why) is: |
| How did the poem sound when it was read aloud? |
| What would be a good subject for the poet to try next? |
| What would be a good form for the next poem? |

*Illustration © 2003, Mary Hall.*

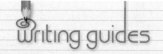

Writing guides

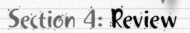

# Teacher review

| | AF5 Vary sentences for clarity, purpose and effect. | AF6 Write with technical accuracy of syntax and punctuation in phrases, clauses and sentences. | AF3 Organise and present whole texts effectively, sequencing and structuring information, ideas and events. | AF4 Construct paragraphs and use cohesion within and between paragraphs. | AF1 Write imaginative, interesting and thoughtful texts. | AF2 Produce texts which are appropriate to task, reader and purpose. | AF7 Select appropriate and effective vocabulary. | AF8 Use correct spelling. |
|---|---|---|---|---|---|---|---|---|
| **LEVEL 1** | Use simple phrases and clauses for effect. Beginning to create sentences by joining clauses using connectives. | Clauses are mostly grammatically accurate. Some correct use of full stops and capital letters. | Events sequenced in appropriate order as poem progresses, *e.g. in counting poems.* Organisation of text generally appropriate to genre, *e.g. regular verses, repetition.* | Some events and ideas linked by repetition of words/phrases to enhance flow of poem. | Information about characters and events portrayed by vocabulary, *e.g. use of nonsense words for places.* Some simple descriptive vocabulary enhances specific elements such as humour/emotion. | Some key features of poetry used in own poems. | Use of simple appropriate vocabulary with some effective word and sound choices. Some humour injected through repetition and rhyming words and sounds, *e.g. bicycle/icicle.* | Some high frequency words spelled correctly. Some attempts to spell nonsense words and sounds phonetically. |
| **LEVEL 2** | Some variation in sentence opening to suit the poem structure, *e.g. repetition of first word on alternate lines.* Simple sentence structure with some use of *and* and *but* as connectives to link lines. Generally consistent use of past and present tenses. | Sentence demarcation using full stops and capital letters generally accurate. Some accurate use of exclamation marks and question marks for poetic effect. | Some simple sequencing of ideas, e.g. dividing common aspects of subject into verses. Opening of verses sometimes signalled by varied presentation techniques, *e.g. bold capitals.* Some correct use of poetic form, *e.g. limericks.* | Planning frames used to connect ideas. Some events and ideas linked by repetition to enhance overall effect of poem. | Content and ideas usually relevant with repetition used to appropriate effect. Features from favourite poems explored together sometimes apparent in own poems. | Some attempts at an appropriate style for genre. General awareness of key features shown. | Some adventurous word choices and introduction of nonsense words for effect. Increasingly effective rhyme choices. | Most high frequency words spelled correctly. Spelling of unknown and made-up words demonstrates increasing knowledge of word structure and spelling patterns. |

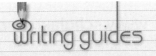

# Also available in this series:

ISBN 978-1407-11253-4

ISBN 978-1407-11265-7

ISBN 978-1407-11267-1

ISBN 978-1407-11256-5

ISBN 978-1407-11270-1

ISBN 978-1407-11248-0

ISBN 978-1407-11254-1

ISBN 978-1407-11266-4

ISBN 978-1407-11258-9

ISBN 978-1407-11268-8

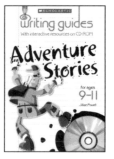
ISBN 978-1407-11251-0

ISBN 978-1407-11257-2

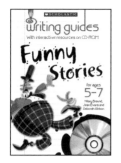
ISBN 978-1407-11255-8

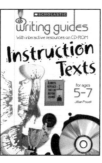
ISBN 978-1407-11269-5

ISBN 978-1407-11250-3

ISBN 978-1407-11247-3

ISBN 978-1407-11252-7

ISBN 978-1407-11264-0

ISBN 978-1407-11249-7

ISBN 978-1407-11260-2

ISBN 978-1407-11261-9

ISBN 978-1407-11263-3

ISBN 978-1407-11259-6

ISBN 978-1407-11262-6

To find out more, call: **0845 603 9091** or visit our website: **www.scholastic.co.uk**